HOW TO DEAL WITH TOXIC PARTNERS

NARCISSISTS, SOCIOPATHS, PSYCHOPATHS

A Solid Guide That Will Help You Regain Control

and Repair Your Relationship

by

Marie Lou

Thank you for purchasing this book. No part of this book may be reproduced, scanned or distributed in any manner without written permission from the author, except in case of brief quotations used in books, articles or newspapers. Your support and respect for the property of this author is appreciated.

This publication contains the opinions and ideas of its author. It is sold with an understanding that the author is not engaged in rendering medical, health or any kind of personal professional services in this book.

This book is intended as reference only, not as a medical manual. The author shall not be liable or responsible for any loss or damage allegedly arising from any information or suggestion in this book.

Copyright © 2016 Marie Lou

All rights reserved.

ISBN-13: 978-1523847808

ISBN-10: 1523847808

CONTENTS

1. Basic Overview Of Personality Disorders: Narcissists, Sociopaths, Psychopaths 1

2. Are You Vulnerable to Manipulation? Warning Signs to Look Out For 6

3. The Narcissists: Main Characteristics and The Way They Operate 12

4. When You Find Yourself In a Relationship With a Narcissist. 17

5. The Sociopaths: Main Characteristics and The Way They Operate 22

6. When You Find Yourself In a Relationship With a Sociopath. 28

7. The Psychopaths: Main Characteristics and The Way They Operate 32

8. When You Find Yourself In a Relationship With a Psychopath............38

9. Dysfunctional Relationships: Emotional, Verbal, Physical and Sexual Abuse............41

10. Is Your Partner Toxic? Take The Test to Find Out............51

11. Repair your Relationship: Necessary Steps to Regain Control And Build a Healthy Relationship 58

| 12 | When You Leave a Toxic Partner Behind: Moving Forward And a Path to Recovery .... 67 |

Frequently Asked Questions..................................... 73

References..78

Resources..79

BASIC OVERVIEW OF PERSONALITY DISORDERS:

NARCISSISTS, SOCIOPATHS, PSYCHOPATHS

Personality disorders are a category of mental illnesses that make a person think and behave in a manner that is out of the ordinary and is inexplicable and inflexible for their societal context. While no one can pin point for sure what causes personality disorders, psychologists and psychiatrists generally believe that experiences from childhood, biochemical imbalances, as well as genetics, play a role in the development of personality disorders. Within individual disorders, the severity also varies greatly with extremely severe cases being completely unable to function while mild disorders are hardly detectable.

One of the factors that aggravates all disorders is the inability of the person with the disorder to realize and accept that he/she has a problem. A narcissist, a sociopath and a psychopath all tend to think there is nothing wrong with their actions and thought processes. While different disorders manifest differently, all will be characterized by inflexibility, whereby one is unable and, in most cases, unwilling to change their behavior and thinking to align with societal norms. A person with a personality disorder, therefore, finds it hard to engage with other people and will, therefore, be withdrawn.

Personality disorders are the most common diagnoses in psychiatric patients with between 40% and 60% suffering one or more disorder. In a considerable percentage of cases, personality disorders overlap: for example, a narcissistic psychopath has both the attributes of a narcissist and a psychopath. The disorders in general inhibit an individual's ability to function within society as a result of their behavior, which may be considered socially distressing. Consequently, their education, careers and relationships suffer. The dark triad of personality disorders encompasses narcissism, psychopathy and sociopathy, which are all characterized by callous manipulative interpersonal style. Below, you'll find basic overview of these common disorders.

Narcissistic Personality Disorder.

Narcissistic personality disorder affects around 1% of the global population. This disorder is characterized by a strong sense of self-importance, individualism and a desperate need for constant affirmation and admiration. This is accompanied by inability to show empathy for others. The result is ego centric, demanding behavior consistent with cluster B of disorders (dramatic, erratic or emotional disorders) as laid out by the American Psychiatric Association in Diagnostic and Statistical Manual of Mental Disorders (DSM-5). Arrogant body language, bragging, criticism and know-it-all attitudes are all behaviors common with narcissists.

A person with a version of narcissistic personality disorder that is less extreme is referred to as narcissist. Many psychology researches have shown a link between narcissistic personality disorder and early childhood environments that may have been inconsistent and un-empathic. Though being a narcissist can sometimes be confused with having a healthy self-esteem and confidence, it actually signifies the opposite. While a narcissist portrays a persona of greatness, it is many times a farce to mask deep insecurities, low self-esteem and feelings of inadequacy. In most cases people with narcissistic personality disorder only seek treatment once they develop symptoms of depression due to perceived criticism, lack of admiration and rejection.

Characteristics of narcissistic personality disorder, according to the DSM-5 include:
· Arrogance and expectations of unreasonable advantages and favors.
· Fantasies of success, fame and power.
· Deep sense of superiority, often viewing others as mediocre.
· Feelings of jealousy and envy.
· Hypersensitivity to insults, imagined or real.
· Inability to acknowledge and empathize with the feelings and needs of others.
· More vulnerable to shame than guilt.

Psychotherapy seeks to address narcissistic personality disorder by improving the individual's perception of reality and their consequent responses to environmental and social triggers.

Psychopathic Personality Disorder.
Psychopathy is an antisocial personality disorder characterized by bold, disinhibited antisocial behavior and diminished or total lack of empathy or remorse. Psychopathy as a diagnosis is not sanctioned by psychiatric and psychological associations, however the term is used widely in criminal justice and in media to define people with certain behavioral characteristics. The relationship between psychopathy and violent crime, sexual abuse (including child

molestation), organized crime and economic crime is strong, given that many psychopaths are amoral with absolutely no regard for moral beliefs.

Causes of Psychopathy.

Unlike narcissistic personality disorder, the probable causes of psychopathy range from genetics and environmental causes to biochemical imbalances. The lack of empathy and remorse in a psychopath is attributed to underdevelopment in the part of the brain that is responsible for emotions and impulse control. Despite depiction in media, psychopaths and sociopaths are not necessarily calculating criminals. However, psychopathy is still considered the most dangerous of all the personality disorders due to the ability of a psychopath to dissociate emotionally with what they do, coupled with their ability to mimic emotions and lead lives that appear to be normal.

Sociopathic Personality Disorder.

According to the American Psychiatric Association's Diagnostic and Statistical Manual of Mental Disorders (DSM-5), sociopathy is also an Antisocial Personality Disorder. As the name implies, the origins of sociopathy are often negative sociological factors such as poor upbringing, parental neglect, physical and emotional abuse, belief systems, delinquent peers or childhood trauma. Though there are high functioning sociopaths who have learnt adaptive skills, most sociopaths live reclusive lives on the fringes of society.

A sociopath behaves impulsively and erratically, but in some instances has the capacity to feel remorse and guilt for their actions. The behavior pattern of a sociopath changes from one extreme to another for no apparent reason.

Many times, the term sociopath and psychopath have wrongly been used interchangeably. While they do have their similarities, there are subtle differences with a huge impact on understanding, diagnosing and treatment.

Nature vs. nurture:

The difference between a psychopath and a sociopath addresses the question of nature vs. nurture. While psychopathy is a result of genetics and biochemical imbalances, many psychologists acknowledge that sociopathy can be acquired as a result of the prevailing circumstances, especially during childhood, in addition to being congenital.

Hot head vs. cold heart:

When it comes to actions and behavior, sociopaths are erratic and impulsive, while psychopaths are manipulative and calculating. Consequently, sociopaths are more likely to live a disrupted life without close relationship ties, while psychopaths are able to lead a semblance of a normal life, despite the fact that psychopathy is significantly more extreme than sociopathy.

Help and treatment:

Personality disorders are illnesses; they, therefore, have causes and treatments. Psychologists and psychiatrists have over time developed therapies and medication that help narcissists, psychopaths and sociopaths adapt to society and lead lives that are almost normal.

In the following chapters we will discuss each one of these disorders, as well as strategies to use if your partner suffers from one of them. We will also discuss ways to defend yourself and repair your relationship; situations when it's best to leave a toxic partner behind; how to heal and move on to a happy love life.

ARE YOU VULNERABLE TO MANIPULATION?

WRNING SIGNS TO LOOK OUT FOR

Manipulation is the process of trying to change another person's behavior, beliefs or feelings by using indirect tactics. It is come for almost everybody to manipulate another at some point. However, there are those, who seem to have perfected this art. In relationships, the manipulative type may greatly manipulate the other partner. These types of people are always determined to have their way. They also fully manipulate to ensure that their weaknesses and mistakes are not revealed. It is, therefore, important to be on the lookout for warning signs of such partners.

In case you are concerned that you are overly manipulated or controlled, you will need to examine the tactics your toxic partner is using. A manipulative partner will often depict traits of a sociopath, a psychopath or a narcissist. They will be highly deceptive and hold unclear intentions and motives. Let us go over common signs and behaviors these partners will use to advance their cause.

Playing the Victim.

What apparently sells these toxic partners is how they play the victim. Even in situations where they have been unfair or overbearing to their partners, manipulators will cry victim. There is the tendency to blame the other person and behave as if they are the ones who have been wronged. A manipulative partner will then go on to cry foul, demand apology or refuse to do his or her part in the relationship.

Telling Lies.

To advance his or her cause, the manipulative partner will greatly depend on peddling lies. Once one lie is either detected or becomes insufficient, another one will quickly be formulated. It is often a lie after another. If your partner is a pathological liar, it could be an indication that he or she is a skillful manipulator.

Gaslighting.

This refers to the process of pushing another person to high points so as to cause an angry reaction and consequently blame the person for the response. Manipulative people will engage in arguments, cruel teasing and scolding to elicit angry feelings. They will then blame the other party for being angry or overreacting.

The Blame Game.

A manipulative partner is full of blame. There is the tendency to blame his or her partner for failures, weaknesses and various occurrences. Such a person will always find a reason to put the blame elsewhere and play the saint. Outsiders or situations outside control take the blame for virtually everything. The victim will be blamed the most for everything happening or not happening.

Pretending to Show Weird Feelings and Acts.
A manipulative person is a perfectionist in pretending to show feelings of guilt, shame, pain, embarrassment and confusion. This is often a way of reacting to the partner or when his or her actions misfire. These are fake emotions merely used to cheat their partners. They are neither genuine nor real. This makes confronting a manipulator a bigger risk to be manipulated further.

In most cases, you will realize that your manipulative partner knows you well. Such a person knows best your strengths and weaknesses. The person will then use your weaknesses to belittle, manipulate and arm-twist you into always doing what he or she wants. Such relationships are then mostly controlled by one person who directly or indirectly runs the show. A manipulative lover is also a professional narcissist. Such person will even go to a point of defending some actions and behaviors by claiming to serve a higher religious or political cause. It is common to find them invoke the name of God or a political figure in justifying their evil or controlling acts.

Now, let's go over the most common character traits that make you an easy target of manipulation and how to avoid that.

Low self-esteem.
Relationship partners who are often easily manipulated mostly have issues with their self-esteem. There is a sinking feeling of worth and acceptance. They will also lack confidence in their abilities and physical appearance. Such people always feel they are unworthy and will even think their manipulative partners are doing them a favor by sticking around. The toxic partner then uses this low self-esteem to manipulate further and control their significant other.

Naivety and ignorance.

Have you ever wondered why your manipulative partner seems to control you so easily? This may have to do with naivety and ignorance. A naive person is easy to sway and control. No wonder there's a saying "knowledge is power". The more informed and exposed you are, the less likely your partner will be to take advantage of you and manipulate you like a marionette.

Dependency syndrome.

A manipulative partner knows best how to use the other partners' dependency to influence and manipulate them. The dependency can be either material or non-material. There is often the issue to either conform or suffer the withdrawal of the support and love. The partner then quickly becomes a soft target for manipulation. Being independent will, therefore, reduce the chances of one being a natural prey for manipulation.

Low assertiveness.

A person who lacks a firm stand is easily manipulated. The ability to agree or disagree and stick to your decision is vital in tackling manipulations. Little assertive ability makes one easily swayed and manipulated by a partner in the relationship. Being confident and firm in one's stand will, therefore, be a shield against unfair manipulation.

Greed and materialism.

Greedy and materialistic partners are easy targets for manipulation. They often believe that by sticking around and being pushed around by their manipulative partners, they may end up benefiting materially. Such people end up doing anything the manipulator wants and will go to a great length to please their toxic partners. In most cases, their partners will never get satisfied.

Fear of negative emotions.
Easily manipulated partners in a relationship often fear negative feelings either from within or from their partners. These emotions include sadness, anger, grief and hate. They, therefore, try to conform to manipulation only to control these fears. They are also likely to fear arousing these negative feelings in their partners.

If you find that you posses some of these traits that make you an easy target for a manipulative partner, the tips below will help you to eventually stop being manipulated.

Be assertive.
Do not be afraid to take a firm stand. Stick to what you believe is right and do not give in to any form of manipulation by your partner. If you persist in your position, it is highly likely that your manipulative partner will learn to respect your stand and stop manipulating you. Avoid being shameful or afraid in doing what you want to do.

Be bold.
Do not allow your manipulative partner to threaten you with veiled threats. Stand up to the person and boldly ask what he or she will do in case of non-compliance. Whenever a threat ensures, be bold and ask about it. Manipulators will thrive by hiding their motives. Only boldness can unveil such intentions. You also ought to be bold in doing what you believe is right.

Be direct and honest.
You must come out strongly and clearly in ending this manipulative game. Clearly state to the manipulative partner that you do not like the manipulation and demand for it to end. That way, the toxic partner will realize how minimal his chances are in manipulating you. However, do not show how

the manipulation makes you feel because your partner can later use it against you.

THE NARCISSITS:

MAIN CHARACTERISTICS AND THE WAY THEY OPERATE.

It is quite common to hear that someone is a narcissist, or even to self proclaim it today. This is because narcissism is often confused with confidence and pride. However, this disorder is more complex. True narcissists are overly confident without merit and are destructive to those around them. Research has shown that most narcissists are men. That is, that 75% of all narcissists are men and the rest are women. These are people with an exaggerated view of themselves. Their ideas of superiority are often unrealistic. It is common, for example, for a highly successful person to proclaim their success. This lack of humility, however, does not make them a narcissist. There are a number of characteristics which all narcissists share. A brief description is provided below.

Exaggeration of self-importance and achievements.
The individuals believe that they, and their work, are extremely important. They may even speak of how they achieve everything on their own. They believe that others in

their surroundings are incapable and holding them back. For example, they have a job of medium importance but will claim that the company will fail without them. A narcissist will also over emphasize the importance of their achievements. For those who do not know the narcissist for a longer period of time, these stories may even seem true. There is never any evidence to prove their importance, but the narcissist will never admit to it.

Sense of entitlement.

The narcissist believes that they deserve recognition and admiration to an exaggerated degree. However, they rarely do anything worthy of such praise. Nevertheless, they demand constant admiration. Even if they receive praise, it is rarely up to their expectations. They also have this sense of entitlement when it comes to favors or wishes. If their wishes are not met, they feel wronged. For example, they expect that people around them will do as they say without question. Another example is feeling entitled to a promotion, even though they do not deserve one. If their needs are not met they feel cheated, and accuse the other person of being unfair or selfish.

Superiority complex.

Such person strongly believes they are better than almost everyone. They will interact only with people who are highly intelligent, successful or otherwise exceptional. In time, they may view themselves as better than these individuals as well. The narcissist dismisses opinions of others and is known to interrupt without hesitation. They believe that only their opinion is correct and relevant. They rarely listen to anyone and prefer to be at the center of every discussion. A narcissist also doesn't take criticism well. They will react aggressively and hurt the other person on an emotional level.

Lack of empathy.

This is the most relevant trait of a narcissist. Lack of empathy means that they can't relate to the pain or happiness of others. Although they do understand that they have hurt someone, guilt or shame for their actions eludes them. This is, in part, because of their self-righteousness and also because they do not understand or feel the full spectrum of human emotions. Therapists claim that their narcissistic patients often feel numb. This lack of empathy means that they cannot connect to anyone on a deeper level.

Envy.

A narcissist not only envies others and their lives or belongings, but also needs to be envied. They will always aim to have the best and the greatest assets in order to be envied. Their own envy and jealousy is always connected to their need to compete with others. If their friend, for example, has a new phone, they must instantly have the same or a better one. This, of course, they believe will make others envy them. They also believe that everyone is jealous of them even if that is not the case.

Desire to always be in control.

Narcissist will often try to control their partner's emotions. Since they feel more important than others, their own feelings are the most important in the relationship. It is extremely difficult to be with the person who doesn't have high regard of their romantic partner.

They are deceitfully charming.

Narcissists are very charming by nature, so they will show genuine interest in their partner at first. After they get hooked, narcissist's focus shifts back on themselves and they will try to manipulate the other person into keeping them pleased at all times.

Feelings of insecurity.
In reality, their insecurities fuel their tendencies to be narcissistic. They will put their partner down and make them feel less adequate or intelligent just because they have to feel they are better. Also, they will try to make sure they are always superior in the relationship.

Now, let's take a look at narcissistic relationship and how it progresses. A narcissistic relationship is any relationship with one or two narcissists involved. They pick and choose a potential partner that is beautiful, successful, rich or otherwise popular. As they only love themselves, they view the people in their lives as possessions. As with all possessions, the goal is to be envied and further praised.

Narcissists have a set routine of how they behave in a relationship:

The courtship.
The first step is that they charm and impress the person they are interested in. The next thing they always do is place this person on a pedestal. The narcissist becomes infatuated with that person and gives them an excessive amount of love and attention. They pay close attention to what their love interest wants in order to manipulate them. This allows them to become the perfect man or woman.

The actual relationship.
Once they are sure that their partner is secured, it seems like they lose interest. They become distant. They stop returning calls and ignore their companion. This leaves the other person feeling rejected and confused. The confusion happens because this transition can happen over night. The love that they felt before was so strong that the target cannot understand what happened. As the other person continues to try and revive the love, the narcissist rejects and hurts them

even more. At some point they start to belittle and blame the other person in every way. Narcissists always scare the people they are involved with. The unfortunate target either becomes defensive or loses confidence in themselves.

The end of the relationship.

The end of the relationship is usually the most damaging to the other person. There are two ways a narcissistic relationship can end. Either the narcissist moves on to someone new, or the other person finds the strength to leave. Whatever happens, the target always wonders what went wrong and whether they were loved. The truth is that no, a real narcissist is not capable of love. Although the introductory phase of the relationship felt like love, it was only infatuation until boredom set in. In most cases, a narcissist will continue to return to their ex for help or reconciliation. They can easily convince their targets that they have changed and that it will be better this time. They rarely change, and it rarely gets better. They simply repeat the process of deep love, boredom, emotional abuse and abandonment.

Conclusion.

While it is hard to realize someone is a narcissist, you can do it if you know the signs and behavioral patterns. With that knowledge they can be avoided. Avoidance is the best strategy, as true narcissists do not feel any of the emotions we may hope that they do. This means they rarely change, as they usually never feel the need to. A narcissistic relationship is a damaging one. These relationships last long enough to leave lasting negative feelings. A narcissist cannot have a meaningful relationship with anyone they meet. Their lack of empathy and vast amount of self-love will always leave them in need of new people to manipulate. They are usually fun, attractive and charming. This, however, wears off and their true, negative side quickly surfaces.

WHEN YOU FIND YOURSELF IN A RELATIONSHIP WITH A NARCISSIST

Even though some people will try to refute it, there is a small part of narcissism in everyone. This is the reason why it is so difficult to know the extent to which someone is narcissistic unless you get to know them better. This is why it is so common to find people realizing that they are repulsed by the narcissistic tendencies of their partners yet they are the same ones, which attracted them in the first place. Therefore, even if you are in a romantic relationship with a narcissist, it does not necessarily mean that you can't love them. These people also have good traits such as great charisma, fun-loving attitude towards life and they are good at what they do. However, if the narcissist in your life brings you more heartbreak than joy, having the right strategies to defend yourself to make your relationship better or to minimize their manipulative nature is of utmost importance.

Consequently, if you are looking for ways on how to deal with the narcissist in your life, there are several strategies you can use.

Establish the type of narcissistic partner you are dealing with.

As you might have already figured out, most narcissists have low self-esteem. Unlike grandiose narcissists, vulnerable narcissists are introverted and you might not realize it when they begin getting in your way or start undercutting you. Thus, you need to determine which type of toxic partner you are in a romantic relationship with to be able to determine which approach to use when dealing with them.

- **Vulnerable narcissistic partner:** He or she will be self-centered and self-absorbed to mask their inner core weakness.
- **Grandiose narcissistic partner:** He or she will have a firm belief in their greatness — though at times they will actually be great.

Accept your annoyance.

If your narcissistic partner often becomes antagonistic and always gets under your skin, you need to accept your annoyance with their mannerisms in order to be able to find ways on how to best deal with them. This is because if you are always trying to outshine your toxic partner, chances are that you will only become more frustrated and annoyed with each passing day.

Appreciate the source of their behavior.

If you are in a romantic relationship with a narcissist, you should realize that your significant other will always try to undercut you and be sneaky as that is their nature. This means that they will question your authority in order to stir some mischief. By recognizing his/her insecurities, you will be able to provide the necessary reassurance to calm him/her down and get them to focus on the relevant matters at hand.

However, you shouldn't give them too much reassurance, as this will fan their ego.

Evaluate the context.

Unlike popularly viewed, narcissism is not a get all or get nothing personality trait. Some events or occurrences will elicit greater insecurities than others. Thus, if you are in a romantic relationship with a narcissist, you should try not to praise someone else over and over again while with them. This is because it will only flare up their emotions, making them become vindictive, spiteful and defensively narcissistic. By evaluating the context of every situation, you should be able to know what and what not to do or say when in a romantic relationship with them.

Be positive.

If your partner usually derives pleasure from seeing others suffer, you shouldn't encourage their behavior. This means that whenever this happens, you shouldn't appear to be ruffled or even annoyed since with time, this behavior will diminish if he/she sees that you are not moved by their actions. In fact, by also following the other strategies along with this one, you will be able to ease the situation so that things can become better.

Avoid getting derailed.

Since your partner will at times try to take center stage and control what you do, you shouldn't give in to their demands. You should try and strike a balance between moving ahead in the direction you want and alleviating your toxic partner's insecurities and anxieties. However, if your partner is a grandiose narcissist, you may consider acknowledging their feelings and then moving on.

Have a good sense of humor.

In as much as calling your narcissistic partner's bluff may mean that you will ignore them, it also means that you will need to meet that bluff with a smile or laugh once in a while. Without being rude, you can simply point out their crude behavior with a joke. This is particularly essential if you have a grandiose type of toxic partner, as he/she will find it amusing and probably instructive.

Recognize their need for assistance.

If your significant other has a low self-esteem and has lots of feelings of inadequacy, you might need to seek professional intervention. This is because even those with long-standing behaviors can change with proper help. More so, tackling their issues yourself might not be feasible.

Regain or protect your independence.

Usually, narcissists tend to make you dependent on them. If you can, you should try and retain some of your independence, as this will make your toxic partner respect you. More so, it might even make him/her become dependent on you to some extent, for instance, if you take on the procurement responsibility.

Check on their willingness to change.

In as much as this might seem obvious, it is very crucial that you evaluate your partner carefully. You could, for instance, ask him/her if they are open to the idea of the both of you seeing a couple's therapist. If they agree, it will indicate that they are ready to change for the better and work on improving your romantic relationship.

Therefore, in as much as your narcissistic partner will at times upset or depress you, you should focus on applying correct strategies of dealing with them to make your romantic relationship balanced. This is because describing what you are going through to others might not give you the satisfaction you need. More so, your family members might not be inclined to believe you, when all they see is a charming partner. Consequently, by using the above strategies to deal with your toxic partner, you can be able to improve your relationship for the better, especially if you have children in the mix, whose well being is of utmost importance.

THE SOCIOPATHS:

MAIN CHARACTERISTICS AND THE WAY THEY OPERATE.

Many writers, journalists, and the general public confuse a sociopath with a psychopath. These two anti-social personality disorders are very different. Unlike a psychopath, a sociopath is able to feel some empathy, even love. Sociopaths have the ability to feel shame, while psychopaths do not. They are also not conniving or calculative, which a psychopath is at all times. They lack the self-control of a psychopath as well. What makes them similar is that both are manipulative and can be dangerous.

Before we go any further, it is first necessary to identify if your partner is a sociopath. How can you tell? Sociopathy is one of the most complex psychological disorders, as it is not limited to one single trait, but rather presents itself as a syndrome. Sociopaths have no regard for others' feelings. Though they are antisocial, they must not be immediately thought of as criminals. Not all sociopaths work against social norms. Rather, they are often very prominent figures, who uphold the law in front of others without fail.

The sociopath is a charming, intelligent and very eloquent individual. They are popular amongst friends and colleagues and can monopolize the conversation. They do this with great stories about their lives, or even jokes. They are known to entertain a crowd and leave a good first impression. Most people have a positive opinion of them, unaware of their sociopathic tendencies. Sociopaths use their knowledge and charm to manipulate those around them. They will also lie in a relationship to not lose fights, keep their needs and demands above anyone else's and manipulate others to do their bidding.

Below are the main characteristics that will help you determine whether you are, in fact, dealing with a sociopath.

They are popular individuals.
Sociopaths have a group of close friends, which idolize them. This group of friends trusts them and believes everything they say. These people have been manipulated and to some extent brain-washed. The sociopath uses this group to achieve specific goals or have their needs met. These may include money, home, or a positive reputation. As with all anti-social disorders, sociopaths view people as tools or objects. Each person serves a purpose. They use this popularity as a mask as well. They can hide in this group, and use these people to speak on their behalf when attacked or accused. Their friends fully believe the sociopath, to the point that they would defend them even if the sociopath is clearly at fault.

They are expert story-tellers and habitual liars.
People with this disorder have a need to embellish everything they say. When telling a story, they will lie in such a way that even the most illogical story will seem possible. These lies can be used to manipulate the audience, or simply to exalt the sociopath. When telling these tales, they make

sure that no one listening was present at the actual event. This is because while their stories hold some truth, the rest is fabricated. Since no one was there, no one can actually claim that they are lying. If someone does bring evidence to prove otherwise, the sociopath will become aggressive, sometimes to the point of violence.

They are reckless and irresponsible.

While most sociopaths are highly intelligent, they are also irresponsible. This may mean that they cannot keep a steady job, or be financially responsible. They disappoint those around them on a regular basis. Naturally, when confronted they offer excuses and blame, but never remorse. This may also be connected to the fact that they have no concern for the emotions of others. They are also reckless to the point of harming themselves. This is interesting as they view themselves as superior or as more important than others. In a way, they are capable of disappointing themselves as well. This may be due to their inability to plan ahead. At some point, they lose control of their reckless idea because they don't think things through. When problems arise, they have no solution. They often put their family and friends in the middle of these careless ideas. Most cult leaders have been known sociopaths. They would also start with an idea that was not well planned. That would cause the idea to crumble, and the sociopath to lose control. In these cult cases, that would often end with mass suicide.

They don't have a conscience.

They have a lack of understanding between right and wrong. This means that most sociopaths engage in some form of criminal activity. Due to their manipulative skills and eloquence, they often commit fraud. They will also steal but rarely for financial gain. Sociopaths can also be aggressive and violent. They have short tempers and little regard for the consequences. When confronted by their loved ones, or by the law enforcement, they have an explanation for everything. They again either fabricate the truth masterfully or blame others for their crimes. Their inability to learn from their mistakes even when punished makes them repeat offenders.

Sociopaths are often unable of having long-term relationships. They become involved with a partner easily, but they rarely stay in a relationship for long. They can, however, form an attachment to another person, but not in a normal way. They will be kind and empathetic one day, and distant another. Their interest in another person comes and goes on a daily or weekly basis. That being said, they can have committed relationships, even get married and have a family.

The beginnings of a relationship with a sociopath.

Sociopaths are usually introduced to their potential partners through family and friends. This is another way that their popularity works in their favor. Their friends can vouch for them. The sociopath is also very charming and can create an ideal image of themselves. They can read a person's needs and wants so well that they can act them out at will. Their great first impressions grab the interest of the possible partner. The beginning of the relationship is always filled with love and excitement. The sociopath may even feel that way about their partner. The sociopath will be kind, loving and attentive. At this point, they gain the full trust of their partner.

The actual relationship.

Once the relationship is secure, the sociopath suddenly changes. They are no longer devoted, kind and loving towards their partner. They become impatient and bad tempered. As with all anti-social personalities, they begin to abuse and degrade their partners. Although the abuse of a sociopath is usually verbal, it can be physical. While this is happening, the sociopath continues to manipulate their loved one. The sociopath may convince their significant other that they are, in fact, the victim. It is not uncommon for the partners of sociopaths to apologize without cause. They show some form of affection throughout the relationship but on irregular basis. This leaves their partner always wanting more and hoping they will change. The loved ones of a sociopath continue to hope that they will reach the good side of their partner.

The end of a romantic relationship.
A sociopath feels no remorse. They have a grandiose view of themselves and are incapable of realizing their mistakes. When a romantic relationship with a sociopath ends, it always leaves the partner destroyed. This is because whatever the outcome, whoever leaves first, the sociopath has no remorse. They behave as if their loved one never existed. Most people try to get some closure but are instead left with nothing. The sociopath takes no time to grieve over the loss of a relationship. They just move on to the next person. This is particularly complex when children are involved. Usually, the sociopath will leave them behind in the same manner. It is much harder, however, to convince a child that their parent is broken and that they are not to blame. A sociopath always leaves lasting scars on those who loved them.

Conclusion.
The sociopath is a reckless and irresponsible individual. They are masters of manipulation with no remorse for the damage they cause. They lie about their lives constantly, and if found out – deny and attack the accuser. There is no way to show the sociopath the negative side of their actions. While they do feel and are capable of some love, they can never love anyone more than themselves. Sociopaths

manipulate and con their way through life. More often they are harmful on an emotional level. However, there have been cases where sociopaths posed a danger to the masses. Sociopaths can be well adjusted and successful. However, they can never have a normal relationship with others, romantic or otherwise. If you're involved with a sociopath, they have to be willing to change for the relationship to work.

WHEN YOU FIND YOURSELF IN A RELATIONSHIP WITH A SOCIOPATH

Being in a relationship with a partner who is sociopathic is indeed a very difficult experience. A lot of times people find it hard to trust their partners again after they get hurt. And with sociopaths, you are doomed to get hurt a lot if you let your guard down. But relationships cannot exist with walls. If you have to tiptoe around your sociopathic partner all the time, you will hardly be able to invest in the relationship. Good news is, it is possible to make a relationship with a sociopath last long, as long as you have some strategies to defend yourself.

While it is not easy, being in love with a sociopath can also become satisfying, as long as you manage to find the right balance in your relationship. You will definitely need to remember that your partner is a sociopath, and not doubt yourself. A lot of times people end up believing that their partner might be capable of love and show morally acceptable behavior, but this may never come true. The end result is not so pretty. You must avoid falling into the usual traps and stay vigilant.

Apart from that, there are several strategies that you can use to defend yourself:

Remember that they usually have no conscience. This is one of the hardest facts to digest in a romantic relationship with your sociopathic partner. You feel love and affection; you want to connect with your partner. However, sociopaths feel none of those. That can be very heartbreaking. But you need to see this differently. For most of us, love means something different based on what we perceive as standards. Standards set expectations, and if we come up short we feel guilty. For sociopaths, there is no need for any standard except the question "what do I want right now?" Beyond that, they will never questions their motives. They constantly keep changing decisions, as they are carried by their momentary whims. You will have to accept this, and take it in stride. It will definitely be tough, but if you set your expectations according to what your partner is capable of, you will handle it better.

Do not believe in their flatteries.
Sociopaths are often interested in dominating over people who are down and have low confidence. When we feel stressed, we seek compliments – and this is where the sociopath is going to strike. Do not believe in what your partner says. While it is really nice to receive compliments, flattery will often create a sense of disillusionment. Sociopathic partners often offer flatteries to their victims to manipulate them. When you see your partner being extra affectionate or charming, make sure that you pay close attention to what they are trying to do. This way you can avoid traps that have been laid out carefully.

Respect yourself.
In her book "The Sociopath Next Door" Martha Stout, an American psychologist, discusses the reasons why we

respect others, especially sociopaths. Should you respect others out of fear? Or should you respect them for knowing what is right from wrong, and because they help others instead of manipulating them? We are often taught to stay respectful and not confront people because of their actions. However, if someone is trying to hurt you and emotionally abuse you, you must show confidence and stand up for yourself. Should you confront your sociopathic partner? Should you fight back or seek help from your family and friends to keep you grounded? The answer would vary depending on the circumstances. You must respect yourself to know that the way you are being treated is not fair. You must be assertive. This way, your partner will not be able to victimize you. The moment you become the victim is when you lose the power in the relationship.

Don't let your emotions fool you.

While your sociopathic partner may not feel love the same way you do, how can you stop yourself from being naively in love with him or her? It is quite difficult to be in love with someone and be blindsided by his or her deceits. When in love, our brains release a neurotransmitter called oxytocin. This is nature's way of creating a bond between our offsprings and us. We are chemically affected, and then when we discover we have been lied to, our brains undergo shock. The brain stops responding properly in such a situation, even though we are still in love with our partner. We cannot follow logic, and end up feeling desperate. This gives the sociopathic partner more opportunities to gain control over their lover.

The best strategy here is to try and stay as mentally alert as possible to what is happening. While you may feel love for your partner, you need to keep your brain sharp. Pay attention to your instincts, and expect that there will be a lot of pitfalls that you have to avoid.

Relationships with a sociopath become a hazard to our

well being only when we let them become toxic partners who can hurt us the first chance they get. But if we adequately defend ourselves from their tactics to manipulate and control, we can do much better to strike a balance that is necessary to maintain an effective relationship with them.

THE PSYCHOPATHS:

MAIN CHARACTERISTICS AND THE WAY THEY OPERATE.

Psychopathic personality disorder falls under the category of antisocial behavior. We all have some antisocial tendencies. Psychopaths, sociopaths, and narcissists, however, have them to the highest degree. Although these three disorders are all antisocial personality disorders, they are very different. That being said, the psychopath is the most dangerous to society.

It is quite complicated to determine that someone is a psychopath. This is because they are aware of their antisocial behavior and are very good at hiding it. All antisocial behavior disorders start in early puberty. This gives the psychopath ample time to practice their acting skills. It is also during puberty that they realize their behavior is not normal and frowned upon. This discovery ensures that they are careful not to be discovered. However, they cannot hide their negative traits forever. Below are the main characteristics that will help you determine whether you are, in fact, dealing with a psychopath.

Outward appearance.
All psychopaths have the characteristics of being charming, intelligent and even popular. Most have good jobs and are capable of holding important positions in society. As they are able to manipulate other people, they can mold people's opinion of them to suit their needs. They may have many friends and acquaintances. This is all because they are great actors. They have deliberately learned to mimic the behavior of others. They can imitate gestures, facial expressions, and language to achieve their goals. To the psychopath, the only important thing is to get what they want at any cost.

Disregard for the law and authority.
While popular opinion is that all psychopaths are violent criminals, this is not true. Most psychopaths do not kill people, but may have broken the law is some minor or major way. This is because they have no conscience. While they do understand the laws, they have no moral code. If they feel they must break the law in order to get what they want, they will. They also feel superior to all and any authority figures. Some psychopaths never break the law in any way. However, even these individuals have a lack of understanding between right and wrong.

They lack many emotions.
Like narcissists, they lack empathy. However, it is on a much deeper level. They do not understand human emotions. They may even be unable to recognize fear, pain or anguish in another person's face. They also do not feel many emotions. Shame and remorse are another set of emotions that they lack. That means they are incapable of being sorry. They may pretend to feel any one of these emotions to get what they want, but they are never genuine. Therefore, their behavior is a result of this lack of emotions.

They are methodological in their manipulation.
Once a certain level of trust is established, the psychopath will use subtle and overt manipulation in order to further his or her own self-centered agenda. Lying, which is typically incredibly easy for psychopaths, is the most common manipulative tactic. Often, the psychopathic partner will engage in cheating or sexual promiscuity, partake in reckless spending or gambling, or abuse drugs/alcohol with a complete disregard for the impact of such actions. Meanwhile, the psychopath's partner is left in the dark as they are overcome with doubt, fear, and insecurity in their partner. To make things worse, the psychopathic partner will often feel justified in pursuing such actions, and if challenged, will lash out with physical or emotional abuse.

A person with psychopathic personality disorder plans their manipulation carefully. They will construct a set procedure to get everything they want. They have no regard for whom they may harm in the process. All people, other than themselves, are irrelevant. They also enjoy the power they have over others. Before they start manipulating anyone, they will discover this person's strengths and weaknesses. They will then use this knowledge against the victim. Nothing a psychopath does is accidental.

Their view of self.
These individuals view themselves as superior to others. The fact that they are usually successful only fuels this opinion. As superior, they believe they have a right to treat those beneath them how they please. In case they are wrong, they place blame on others. The fault can never be their own. This overconfidence may seem attractive at first, but soon it is seen as selfish.

Charm.
Commonly, psychopaths are above average in the "courtship" process. In the beginning of the relationship,

psychopaths will trick their partners into thinking that they are principled, possess virtue, and carry a high degree of empathy for others. This facade is meant to gain a necessary level of trust from their partners, which will ultimately serve as the framework upon which the psychopath will abuse and hurt his or her lover. In normal relationships, this trusting bond comes naturally, and arises from a mutual appreciation for one another's strengths and desirable traits. In psychopathic relationships, this bond is entirely one-sided; the psychopath exploits the trust of their partner as a means to manipulate and control, and to satisfy the psychopath's twisted sense of ego and self-worth.

Physical or verbal abuse.
While there has been much research to support the fact that psychopaths tend to have a "shallow" emotional capacity, this doesn't mean that psychopaths are unable to experience emotions. It's important to remember that, while they often lack empathy, psychopaths tend to experience a range of negative emotions such as anger, rage, jealousy, fear, and insecurity. While everyone experiences these emotions to a certain extent, psychopaths often use them as a means of not only gaining power over their partner, but also justifying their abuse. In other words, while most people would feel a tremendous sense of guilt or remorse, the psychopath only feels righteous in his or her devastation. Manifesting in constant criticism or belittlement, overt put-downs, and abandonment, the psychopath breaks down his or her partner to the point of insanity.

Overall, psychopaths are incapable of maintaining a committed relationship. At the same time, their relationships can last long time. They have even been known to get married. This does not mean that those relationships are healthy or monogamous. They will maintain their charming facade to the public, but life at home will be very different.

Psychopaths pick potential partners that are emotionally unstable due to some sort of trauma. Not people with other disorders, but people who find themselves lonely or insecure. They use all their charm and ask as many questions as possible. This does two things. First, it makes the person feel valued and interesting, so they lower their guard. Second, it allows the psychopath access what the victim is looking for. This, in turn, allows them to become the perfect mate. A psychopath will usually pursue a few targets at the same time. Although they choose one that is the most useful to them as a primary mate, they rarely let go of the others.

When a psychopath has their grip on their victim, the abuse begins. This can be psychological, physical, sexual or all three. In the case of marriage, they will trap their significant other with children. They are not capable of any form of love, but will show affection sparsely to keep the other person at all costs. Even their sexual advances are simply to get what they want. Apart from meeting their needs, the psychopath highly values power and control. This affects how they behave when in romantic relationships. They manipulate and humiliate their partner in many ways to maintain control. They will isolate their mate from family and friends. This again preserves their control, but also shows the other person their power. This means that their lover will be unlikely to leave, as they have nowhere to go. Psychopaths do not have relationships to fill a void of any kind. Every relationship has its purpose. Whether with a friend, a wife or a child, psychopath views them as objects to be used.

A psychopath never ends one relationship without having another one reserved. They get bored as soon as the surge of dopamine, which is released in the beginning, subsides. That, however, does not mean they end all relationships quickly. They change many mates, but may have one constant relationship at the same time. In rare cases the significant other leaves. This is rare because the psychopath destroys their self-esteem and independence early on. When this does happen, the psychopath will stalk their ex-lover. They do not accept defeat and view this as such. Even if the antisocial individual was the first to leave, they have a tendency to return. They use all the tools they have learned while being with the victim to reconcile. Of course, they still have no emotions, so the abuse resumes quickly thereafter.

Conclusion.

Unlike many other disorders, a psychopathic one cannot be treated. This is because they have a serious lack of emotions and morals. In order for a person to be treated, they must want to change what's wrong with them. A psychopath believes there is nothing wrong with them. They feel the rest of us are weak for having emotions. Their only goal in life is to serve themselves. What they want and need is the only relevant thing in their lives. With that in mind, they are prepared to do anything to achieve these goals. They have no empathy towards the people they hurt. This means that they will continually abuse people in their lives. Their lack of caring leaves them cold and all the emotions they show are fabricated. This makes the psychopath dangerous to those they meet.

WHEN YOU FIND YOURSELF IN A RELATIONSHIP WITH A PSYCHOPATH

In many relationships, the dynamic between lovers begins harmlessly enough, and often evolves into a loving bond between two equals. However, if one unexpectedly enters a relationship with a psychopath, the initial romance can devolve into a nightmarish mess that seems impossible to escape. Relationships with psychopaths can be traumatic, stressful experiences that lead to tremendous pain and hardship. However, if one is armed with the right tools to defend against a psychopath, one may be able to tolerate the relationship until an ending can be arranged. Psychopaths are initially hard to spot, because they often do an outstanding job at presenting themselves as charismatic, charming, flirtatious, or caring. Beneath the surface, however, psychopaths are anything but. Because of their supremely inflated sense of self-worth and importance, psychopaths tend to see themselves as the center of the universe. Combine that with an inability to empathize or show remorse, and you have a potentially deadly combination. While many psychopaths manifest their actions in outright criminal behavior, others exercise their devastation in subtler ways, wreaking havoc in their romantic lives. What, then, does it mean to call someone a "psychopath" in the context of relationships? In an article posted in "Psychology Today," the author notes that, "[The Psychopath's] hallmark is a stunning lack of conscience; their game is self-gratification at the other person's expense... The most obvious expressions of psychopathy – but not the only ones – involve the flagrant violation of society's rules." In other words, the psychopath shares many common traits of a sociopath, exercising an utter lack of empathy and disregard for the well-being and feelings of his or her partner in order to better himself or herself. With manipulation, charm, aggression, physical or verbal abuse, pathological lying, and a lack of empathy, the psychopath often views the relationship as a means of dominating or gaining power over his or her partner.

While it seems like a no-brainer that a complete and permanent separation is the best course of action, this isn't always so easy. Consider how effective the Nazis were in brainwashing an entire nation to believe their horrific agenda. Consider the North Korean regime, and how they've led most of their citizens to believe that the United States is a demonic entity with nuclear weapons poised to fire at any minute. Consider the alarming number of individuals that have joined ISIS and other extremist ideologies. Now imagine a partner who's been constantly insulted and belittled for years, separated from family and friends, yet can't seem to let go of their psychopathic abuser. What do all of these examples have in common? Brainwashing, pure and simple. If repeated enough times by a charismatic leader or individual, a twisted perception of reality begins to set in, until it becomes the absolute truth.

Now let's discuss how one can free one's self from this false reality:

1. **Family presence.** Having a supportive and caring family network is critical in terms of helping the victim come to an objective understanding of their present situation. While the psychopath may do

everything possible to trick the victim into thinking that there's no way out, a family that's able to spot a psychopath can educate the victim to the psychopath's selfish and manipulative tendencies.

2. **Counseling.** If the victim is able to seek counseling, he or she should do so at all costs. A counselor may then explain the traits of a psychopath, and ultimately identify the victim's abuser as one. This could go a long way in helping the victim to "snap out" of their misguided state of mind.

3. **Complete separation.** If possible, and if the victim is strong enough, a complete separation from the abuser should be a course of action. Of course this isn't easy, but this is perhaps the only way how one can move on completely from a psychopathic relationship.

Ultimately, being able to identify and separate from a psychopath at the onset of abuse is the most powerful weapon. Unfortunately, many people are incapable of doing so, but with a supportive family network and proper counseling, the victims may ultimately be able to separate from their psychopathic partners, and eventually heal their emotional scars.

DYSFUNCTIONAL RELATIONSHIPS:

EMOTIONAL, VERBAL, PHYSICAL AND SEXUAL ABUSE

Love and relationships are among the most widely discussed issues today, as everybody wants to have the happiest relationship possible. While a relationship can make us happy, it can also make our life miserable if our partner abuses us emotionally, verbally, sexually or physically.

Dysfunctional relationships are those relationships that do not perform their relationship obligation appropriately. What I mean is that one of the partners doesn't support the other. When you are in a relationship with someone you are supposed to feel safe, loved, respected and free to be yourself. As the saying goes, love is not supposed to hurt, but for millions of people in the United States and worldwide, domestic abuse in one or more forms is part of their daily lives. According to domestic violence experts, over 4 million women are victims of domestic assault each year in the United States. Reports from the National Association of Women show that over half a million assaults by intimate partners are reported annually and nearly half of these require hospitalization. The most common form of an abusive relationship is one where the man is the abuser. Men are generally said to be more abusive than women; however, research shows that the rate of abuse is basically the same for both men and women. Here, we will focus on dysfunctional relationships in general, no matter who is the abusive partner. Clearly, domestic abuse is a grim reality, but it does not always come in the most stunning, headline-grabbing fashion. It can be defined as a pattern of abusive and coercive behaviors, used against an intimate partner to maintain power or control over them. Abuse in a relationship is not normal. What most people tend to ignore is the fact that abuse tends to escalate with time. When someone uses abuse and violence against a partner, it ends up being a larger pattern of control. Abuse can be emotional, verbal, physical and sexual, as explained below. Gaining some insight into the different types of the abuse can help you protect yourself.

Emotional abuse.
Also referred to as psychological aggression, emotional abuse can simply be defined as the use of verbal and nonverbal actions, intended to inflict mental harm and affect the well-being of the victim. Nothing can be more damaging to one's self-esteem than being in an emotionally abusive relationship. Emotional abuse, unlike the physical one which rears its ugly head in dramatic outburst, can be more insidious and elusive. In fact, there are cases where neither the abuser nor the victim is aware that it is happening. Emotional abuse can also be defined as a regular pattern of bullying, verbal offense, threatening and constant criticism, as well as other subtle tactics like shaming, intimidation, and manipulation. In those romantic relationships where there is emotional abuse, it is usually a continuous process in which one individual seeks to systematically diminish and destroy the inner self of the other. The victim's essential ideas, perceptions, feelings and personal traits are constantly belittled. Many victims report that it is equally harmful, if not worse, than the physical aggression they suffer.

The scope of what entails as psychological aggression is wide, but below are a few examples:
- Demanding submission to whims
- Ordering the partner around
- Refusing to share in childcare or housework
- Withholding resources (ex. money) and/or affection
- Restricting the partner's mobility and usage of car or phone
- Monitoring the partner's whereabouts and time
- Threatening to walk out of the relationship
- Acting suspicious and/or jealous of the partner's social contacts and friends

Most often, the abusive partner takes charge of everything, including household money and closely monitors all your steps. He or she is always threatening to throw you out or even leave you. They force you to socialize even if you do not feel like it. They also withhold attention or affection and will always dictate your dress code. These types of partners will always ensure that you don't get whatever you want; they must have their way at all times. This type of partner will also make attempts to cause rifts between you and your family members. They also make sure that you spend little time with your friends and that all their friends are your friends as well.

An abusive partner will always blame others for their own shortcomings. They will always be a different person in public as compared to the person at home. When needed, they will twist your own words so that they can use them against you. Abusive partners are disrespectful. They also attempt hurting those that you hold dear to your heart, like your pets. They will roll eyes at you, humiliate you in public and at home.

Most male and female abusers tend to have some kind of personality disorder, such as narcissistic, sociopathic or psychopathic personality disorder. Most victims tend not to see the mistreatment as abusive and they end up developing a coping mechanism of denial and minimizing in order to deal with their stress. However, the long term effects of an emotional abuse are likely to cause severe emotional trauma in the victim including depression, anxiety and post traumatic stress disorder.

Verbal abuse.
When we are talking about domestic abuse our minds mostly drift to external signs such as black eyes, broken bones, bleeding and bruises. However, research shows that long-term effect of verbal abuse can be devastating, if not more serious than that of physical abuse. In basic terms, verbal abuse involves name-calling and yelling. Often, it also forms the basis of nearly all other forms of abuse in romantic relationships.

Verbal abuse is mostly a lie or sometimes a truth that someone tells you about you, what you are, what they think about you and their motives and often leads to emotional or mental anguish. Some of the common types of verbal abuse include threatening, defaming, blaming, trivializing, blocking, countering and diverting. Many women have to endure harsh words from their partners daily, which quietly affects them emotionally and/or mentally. According to relationship experts, verbal abuse usually leads to physical abuse as it escalates.

Some common examples of verbal abuse are:
- Yelling and insulting
- Swearing
- Name-calling
- Ridiculing, berating or belittling

The effects of verbal and emotional abuse intertwine, since the effects of verbal abusive statements greatly affect the victim's emotions. However, some of the prominent effects include confusion, where the victim feels like something is wrong with them, self doubt, low self esteem, fear, depression and stress. In the long run, most victims suffer chronic pain, migraine and persistent headaches, as well as ulcers, spastic colon and frequent indigestion and constipation.

Physical Abuse.
The most common and obvious form of abuse in romantic or sexual relationships is physical abuse. It affects millions of women and girls of all ages across the country. It involves physical aggression or acts of violence intended to cause temporary injury or physical pain to the victim. It ranges from minor acts, such as slapping, to severe acts that cause great injury or even death. Each day, about 4 women die in the U.S due to domestic violence. In fact, the number of women who have died from domestic assault is greater than the number of American soldiers who lost their lives in the Vietnam War.

Physical abuse in a relationship is the use of physical force against someone in a way that it endangers or injures that person. Even though physical abuse often does not result in emotional abuse, emotional abuse often progress into a physical one.

Physical abuse may occur once, sporadically or infrequently, but in most cases, it is recurring and unceasing, and with time, it escalates in severity and frequency.

Some general examples of physical abuse include:
- Biting
- Forced sex
- Beating, punching

- Spitting
- Scratching
- Hair pulling
- Pushing, shoving, grabbing
- Chocking or struggling
- Hitting or slapping with an open hand
- Cutting, scalding or burning

Some of the common effects of physical abuse include: temporary pain, injuries, bruises, broken bones and long-term injuries. Long-term effects of an ongoing physical abuse can put your at the risk of developing a permanent health condition and also lead to disability and even death.

The other long-term effects include:
- Hypertension (high blood pressure)
- Arthritis
- Heart disease
- Sexually transmitted diseases
- Chronic pain syndromes

Sexual abuse.

This is the least obvious form of abuse. It is unfortunate that most couples do not know their rights and they think that since they are in a relationship or married to their spouses, it is their spouse's obvious conjugal right to have sex with them. I will have to clarify this. Any sex without the full consent of the other party is sexual abuse. Sex needs to be consensual. Even though with time rape has mostly been considered the most obvious form of sex abuse, there are other forms of sexual abuse that are less than rape, but equally destructive over time. Some of these include excessive jealousy and derogatory attitude. I categorize these as subtle sex abuse since most people do not recognize them as such.

Sexual abuse is a broad category that encompasses marital rape, rape by cohabitating or dating partner, and rape by someone other than romantic partner. It also involves acts that fall under the legal definition of rape, in additional to physical abuse to the sexual parts of the victim's body, and making sexual demands with which the victim is uncomfortable. Some experts have also defined it as sex without consent, sexual handling of reproductive rights and all types of sexual manipulation, performed by the perpetrator with the intent to cause sexual, physical and emotional harm to the partner. Almost 1.2 million women are sexually abused by their former or current male partner yearly.

Examples of sexual abuse include:
- Demanding sexual intercourse when the partner is unwilling
- Coercing or forcing the partner to participate in sexual activities, with which the partner is uncomfortable
- Attacking physically sexual parts of the partner
- Forced penile penetration of any form (vaginal, anal or oral)
- Coerced or forced sex in the presence of others
- Coerced or forced sexual activity with individuals other than the partner
- Coerced or forced sex with animals

Most sexual abusers see others as being put on earth to satisfy them sexually and, therefore, do not take into account that the victims feel pain when abused. Unfortunately, if the victim agrees to participate in sexual acts with the abuser just for the sake of peace, they risk being further verbally or physically abused for having complied. In most relationships, subtle sex abuse is often used to control, degrade and dominate the victim.

Some of the common effects of sexual abuse include:
- Being sex phobic
- Approaching sex as an obligation
- Getting angry and disgusted with any form of sentimental touch
- Difficulty in getting aroused or having sensational feeling
- Engaging in compulsive or inappropriate behaviors
- Experiencing ejaculatory or erectile difficulties

Some of the notable effects of remaining in a dysfunctional relationship are gradual but steady erosion of self worth. You suddenly wake up one morning and you realize that the only identity you are left with is that which the abuser has chosen for you. It might take a long time to get over the damage done and it is not a surprise to find someone with serious personality disorder as a result of a long and unhealthy relationship.

The other effects include:
- Constant fear of one's partner
- Feeling of being controlled most of the time
- Fear of being rejected by the alleged abuser

- Low self-esteem

It is not abnormal to be in an unhealthy relationship, but what is not normal is when we choose to stay in such relationships. Whenever you feel abused or your relationship is not taking the right course, it is always advisable to seek professional help early enough before the real damage is done.

Breaking Free From an Abusive Relationship.
Interestingly, most psychiatrists and other relationship experts say that virtually all women in abusive relationships are aware of their predicament but often fail to take action due to various factors. Most women do no leave at the first sign of domestic abuse because they do not want to rock the boat, they do not have the social support to leave or they lack the financial resources. Due to the controlling nature of most abusers, it is difficult for most women to contact someone who can help them. It is even tougher to prevent domestic abuse, since most abusers usually do not think they have a problem. The only sure way to protect yourself is to leave at the first sign of such behavior.

You can take the following crucial steps to make sure of your safety:
- If you find yourself in a heated situation with your partner, stay clear of the kitchen (it is reportedly the most common place for domestic violence, perhaps due to accessibility to too many possible weapons).
- Avoid any tiny rooms such as closets or bathrooms, where you can be trapped.
- Call 911 as soon as you are able to.

- If you are hit, get medical attention as soon as you can.
- Take pictures of any injuries to your body or to the children.
- Memorize emergency numbers and try to keep a phone with you at all times.
- Keep a small suitcase packed for you (and your children if any), with important documents such as driver's license, social security numbers and health insurance information.

DO YOU HAVE A TOXIC PARTNER? TAKE THE TEST TO FIND OUT

The test below is developed by Dr. Jeffrey Bernstein, a psychologist with over twenty-five years of experience specializing in child, adolescent, couple, and family therapy. He holds a Ph.D. in Counseling Psychology from the State University of New York at Albany and completed his post-doctoral internship at the University of Pennsylvania Counseling Center. He has appeared on the Today Show, Court TV as an expert advisor, CBS Eyewitness News Philadelphia, 10! Philadelphia – NBC, and public radio.

As you read through the list below, put a mental check mark (or print out this page and get out your pen) next to each toxic thinking pattern you do toward your partner. Even though this list is not an empirically validated formal assessment, you can at least get a sense of how toxic your relationship is by reviewing these nine, common occurring toxic thoughts.

How many of these do you or your partner struggle with?

___**The All-or-Nothing Trap:** You see your partner as either always doing the wrong thing, or never doing the right thing. ("He always has to be right!")

___**Catastrophic Conclusions:** One partner exaggerates negative actions and events concerning the other partner. ("She bounced that check and now we are definitely heading to the poor house!")

___**The "Should" Bomb:** One partner assumes the other will meet one or more of his or her needs – just because he or she should know that need. ("You should know how much I hate my job, even though I tell everyone what a great opportunity it is.")

___**Label Slinging:** You unfairly, and negatively, label your partner and lose sight of his or her positive qualities. ("You are so lazy!")

___**The Blame Game:** You unfairly, and irrationally, blame your partner for relationship issues, or bigger issues. ("My life only sucks because of you!")

___**Emotional Short Circuits:** Emotional short circuits occur when one partner becomes convinced that his or her partner's emotions can't be "handled. ("No one can possibly ever reason with her!")

___**Overactive Imagination:** In this case, you reach negative conclusions about your partner that are not based in reality. ("She's so preoccupied lately; she must be having an affair.")

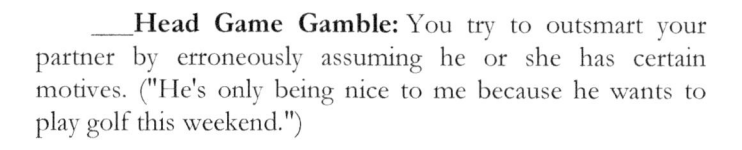

___**Head Game Gamble:** You try to outsmart your partner by erroneously assuming he or she has certain motives. ("He's only being nice to me because he wants to play golf this weekend.")

___**Disillusionment Doom:** This occurs when partners focus on idealized expectations of their partner that are rooted in the past. ("All he does now is worry about his job; he is just like all the other guys who never cared one bit about my needs.")

Happy, satisfied couples that do not get bogged down in toxic thoughts have a better, more realistic and healthy way of thinking about each other. It is this way of thinking that enables such couples to improve communication, solve problems, and enhance romance. This true foundation for a happy relationship, this elusive secret to your success, can only be found, or built, in one place – your own mind.

The following test is adopted from Do Personality Testing1 to find out whether you are in a toxic relationship where emotional abuse is present.

Count the signs that are true for you and your relationship as you go along to get your toxic relationship score.

Low Score: 0-3 Emotional Abuse Signs.
Medium Score: 4-6 Emotional Abuse Signs.
High Score: 7-10 Emotional Abuse Signs.

Sign # 1. Changeable
Your partner changes like the weather. You never know when he's going to be loving and attentive, like he was at first, or mean and distant.

Sign #2. Game Playing
See what happens if you miss one of his/her calls by accident... he/she becomes a major ignoring game-player.

Sign # 3. Controlling
Do exactly as he wishes at all times or else he'll start acting weird on you.

Sign # 4. Passive Emotional Manipulation
He/she gives you the silent treatment for no reason

Sign # 5. Walking on Eggshells
You have to keep secrets from your partner because he/she gets angry even about little things.

Sign # 6. Everyone and Everything Else Comes First.
Taking out the garbage is more important than giving you any attention, even on your birthday.

Sign # 7. No Emotion
He doesn't allow you to express your emotions or to talk about how you feel. It's always about him, his feelings, and what you've done wrong.

Sign # 8. Distant Lover
'Push you, pull you' is their favorite game. He/she pulls your close only to push you away.

Sign # 9. Dismissive
He doesn't listen to you at all. Or when he does pay attention he laughs, saying you don't know what you're talking about.

Sign # 10. Confidence Knocker
He's talking about his amazing ex-girlfriends again. If they weren't models, they were famous.

1. **Emotional Abuse: Low Score**
No / Few Red Flags of Emotional Abuse.

Advice: clear and open communication all the way!
Your score reflects that you are not in a toxic relationship. Although you may at times argue with your partner, it would seem that when a problem arises you have the maturity it takes to talk through your problems in an open and direct manner.

Emotional abuse is present in relationships where needs are not directly expressed by one or both of the partners. Open communication is absent in emotionally abusive relationships because both parties fear rejection as a result of speaking their truth.

The clearest sign of emotional abuse in a relationship is whether the love experience hurts. If a person finds that they cannot function normally while in their relationship due to concern about their drama-filled relationship, then they are likely to be in a toxic relationship.

2. Emotional Abuse: Medium Score
Toxic Relationship: Red Flags Waving High in the Sky
Your love experience is hurting you!

Advice: refuse to be a victim.

Your score suggests that emotional abuse is present within your relationship, which may be causing damage to your sense of self. If your relationship swings between highs and lows, then you may be in a relationship in which emotional manipulation is present.

Your test answers indicate some red flags and warning signs for emotional abuse. The reason for emotional abuse in relationships is because needs and feelings are not being openly and directly expressed. Emotional abusers live in deep fear that if they communicate what they want, they will be in some way rejected for showing a weakness or vulnerability.

An emotionally abusive partner is deeply insecure in relationships and cannot help but constantly test the devotion of their partner by playing games and rejecting them. Such game playing causes stress and anxiety for the victim of the abuse, who over time will have their sense of self eroded.

3. Emotional Abuse: High Score
Toxic Relationship: Red Alert!
You have internalized the idea that love is pain.

Advice: free yourself from the toxic relationship yoke.

Your score suggests that you may be in a toxic relationship in which unhealthy patterns of relating mean that emotional abuse is present. If you find that your love experience traps you in a state of fear regarding the status your relationship, then it is possible that you are being emotionally manipulated by your partner.

Emotional abusers manipulate in relationships because they are not able to directly communicate their needs. They use games and emotional manipulation to gain control over their partners.

While emotional manipulators may on the surface appear powerful and in control, the reality is that they are insecure about the status of the relationship and for this reason continually test their partners with games and challenges. The victim of emotional manipulation will over-time lose their sense of self-worth from being made to feel as if they can do nothing right.

REPAIR YOUR RELATIONSHIP:

NECESSARY STEPS TO REGAIN CONTROL AND BUILD A HEALTHY RELATIONSHIP

People never plan to be in abusive relationships. As a matter of fact, most never realize that they are in an abusive relationship until it's already too late. People who have never been victims of abusive and controlling partners will always have a difficult time understanding how someone can get abused and not realize that. If you are amongst these people, be grateful and do not be judgmental. Controlling and abusive partners will never show their true colors on the first dates. As discussed in previous chapters, they are very affectionate during the embryonic stages of a relationship. This makes the other person rush and make commitments thinking they have found "Mr. or Mrs. Right".

Once you realize you are, in fact, romantically involved with a toxic partner, follow these strategies to regain control.

Recognize the signs.

The first and foremost step is to recognize and accept that you are in a relationship that is abusive. Living in denial is always catastrophic. You may be feeling that your partner is just an overbearing jerk and that he or she is not that bad. It's until you accept that your partner is abusive that you can have better chances of regaining control in such a relationship. Having discussed different types of abuse in the previous chapter, it should be easy for you to realize that your partner is abusing you emotionally, verbally, sexually or physically. Be honest with yourself; don't deny that you are being abused. Recognizing this abuse is the first step to fighting it, keeping in mind that you just can't allow it to continue.

Set limits on your partner's emotional outbursts and criticism.

Make sure that your partner is aware that you are always open to hear their concerns. Make sure that they know how their actions affect you as a person. Let them know that you are no longer comfortable to engage in conversations that attack your personality. If you are a woman, the man that is abusing you may be the only man in the world that you love with all your heart, but this does not mean that you should allow him to make you feel like you are in prison. Let him know that you can even quit the relationship if that will give you peace.

Deal with negative criticism in a positive way.

In most cases, victims of abuse react to their partner's actions or words without thinking of their beliefs first. Listen to your partner's criticism, offensive words and intimidation and try to react to them positively. For example, criticism on the part of your earnings should stimulate you to work harder or in a more innovative way to further your career, instead of having self-pity. This will turn the tables as soon as your partner recognizes that you are actually improving in the aspects that they criticize you on.

Consider your partner's concerns.
What are you willing to offer your partner? Ensure that whatever you want to do for them will be beneficial to both of you. Do not agree to do anything in desperation in order to save your relationship, especially if deep down in your heart you are aware that it is not right for you.

Don't overreact.
Avoid heated arguments with your partner over an abusive behavior at all costs. Arguments will only add an insult to the injury. Instead, do your best not to take things personally and let it go. Practice self-control and above all, respect yourself.

Be honest with yourself first before being honest with your partner.
Consider your needs, goals and values. Ensure that any decision that you make is for your own benefit first. Let your partner know your boundaries; what you can and cannot do for them. Do not be intimidated in whatever you want to do. Whenever you disagree, be clear by having a powerful "No". Be clear that whenever you say "no" they have no option, but to respect your decision. If they cannot respect your decision, it's best for both of you to go separate ways.

Secretly save money.
If your abusive partner is controlling the finances, set up a secret account. If you can't set a secret account, look for a place that is far away from the house and save your own money. For example, you can use your office locker. You can

also give your money to a friend whom you trust to keep your money on your behalf. Another alternative place where you can safely keep your money is inside a safe deposit box. Just in case you receive your paychecks through direct deposits, make sure that some of that cash is transferred to a different account.

Get help.

The biggest mistake that most people, especially women, do is staying in abusive relationships because they always feel embarrassed to tell their family members and friends what's really going on. If they have partners who behave like "Mr. or Mrs. Perfect" when they are in public, they may have a feeling that nobody will believe what they say. In this case, you should also look for help through online resources. You must not allow yourself to undergo this kind of suffering alone.

Get your power back.

The easiest way of doing this is walking away from the relationship if the situation is beyond repair. This will enable to make progress not from a position of weakness, but from a position of strength.

Find people who celebrate who you are.

Look for ways that will assist you in rediscovering yourself. Connect and engage with people who will unconditionally love you and support you irrespective of your shortcomings. It's only you who can make a decision whether to live with your toxic partner or not. You must be in a relationship that supports your growth and not a relationship that puts you down. You have a right to be in a loving relationship; you must, therefore, love yourself. It's always the main step towards regaining control when you are in a relationship with an abusive partner.

Having said that, not all dysfunctional relationships are doomed. It is possible for abusers in a relationship to change if they admit what they have done, stop the blame game and make the necessary amends. This will lead to a healthy relationship with is characterized by love, care and understanding. A healthy relationship involves two people, connected on a deep psychological level. At the same time, each partner is responsible for their own happiness. Together, they make their happiness complete. A partner does not put boundaries on the life of their loved one. Overall, everyone lives life at their own pace.

A healthy relationship is one where each partner recognizes and appreciates the needs of the other. Each partner in a relationship demands something different from the other person. This explains why in most cases, getting the right partner is easier said than done. Women need to respect their men unconditionally. If you are able to give your man unconditional respect, he will be the happiest man in the world. He will be satisfied and content. On the other hand, women need unconditional love from the men in their lives. If you love your woman truly and unconditionally, she will feel as if she owns the world. This way, there is mutual understanding and benefit. In a healthy relationship, every partner works towards its success. Relationships are said to be like a football match, where everybody plays their part to avoid defeat. You have to work hard to ensure that your love life is successful, but you should not give all your life to your partner.

All relationships are as unique as the people in them. This means that there is no exact recipe for happiness. There is no exact number of laughs; there are no exact types of romance. A relationship grows and evolves with the people that make them. That being said, there are certain characteristics of a healthy relationship. These are constant. Keep in mind that people do argue and no one is perfect. A healthy relationship does not mean there are no conflicts within it. Rather, it is about the way two people relate to each other.

There is not one thing that makes a couple work. It is a combination of factors and the way two people unite that creates a good, healthy relationship. The factors, or characteristics, that make a couple work are important. Stress creates conflict and people make mistakes. It is the way a couple deals with problems that dictate the type of relationship they have. Factors such as trust, respect, and understanding are all a part of this. In fact, these following factors should be a set goal for all couples to reach. Above all else, love and the wish to make a relationship great is what makes relationships last.

Respect.
Many psychologists will agree that respect is vital for both the individual and the couple as a whole. In a relationship, it is important that the respect is mutual. Respect is shown in many ways. The wishes and needs of both partners are important. This means that both partners' opinions carry equal weight. In spite of disagreements, they should be able to listen and appreciate what the other is saying. It is also important not to lose the individuals within the relationships. Excessive jealousy and control can force a person to conform to the rules that they don't agree with. When their privacy and character are invaded, the relationship itself suffers. Respecting each other for who they both are and allowing each other privacy is key. Within healthy relationships, both partners appreciate each other's families, obligations and views.

Trust and Honesty.
Trust and honesty go hand in hand. Without one, the other is impossible. In other words, if a person does not trust their partner, they will not be able to be honest. A couple should be honest about many issues. These issues include the

way a person feels, thinks, behaves and so on. Yet this can be complicated. This happens if either or both of them experienced rejection when being honest in the past. This is a process. Couples spend their whole lives trusting and being honest. Despite the fact that people make mistakes, a strong couple is one which can forgive and move forward. This, of course, must be mutual and fair. If one is always forgiving while the other is constantly letting them down, then this is not a healthy relationship.

Communication.
For any relationship to function, good communication skills are needed. Every couple converses in their own way. Some people are more talkative while others are quiet. This is irrelevant. What is relevant is that they understand each other. Within a healthy couple, both partners listen, as well as talk. Even when arguing, they are able to do so with a positive tone. For example, they may disagree about who spent more money, but they do not judge or blame each other. They also do not dismiss or degrade the person they love. An argument in a healthy relationship is more a debate than a fight. They also take the time to explain their thoughts and emotions.

Compromise and boundaries.
It is well known that compromise is a big part of any committed relationship. As with every other aspect mentioned this must be mutual. Any compromise made must not be too great a sacrifice. A loving partner would never ask for this. Instead, the compromise would be one that both partners can live with. It is also fair. If one partner cannot compromise, he or she is not met with aggression. In a healthy relationship, partners to do not threaten each other to get what they want. Throughout the healthy relationship, both partners compromise respectively. This can be something small, like what restaurant to eat at. It can also be

something more important, like who pursues their career first. That being said, there have to be boundaries. Both partners should be able to keep all the things they find important. In a thriving relationship, no one is forced to do anything, and both sides have the right to choose.

Affection, intimacy and friendship.

These three factors complement each other in a healthy relationship. Begin with friendship. There is a difference between a relationship and a friendship. However, make your partner your greatest friend. Some people just rush to the romantic side of a relationship, forgetting the simple things that make a relationship last. You cannot climb a tree from the top. For this reason, it is important to ensure that you are great friends first, so that this friendship can grow into a healthy and loving relationship.

Affection is shown through kind words and compliments. It is also shown through non-sexual touch. This refers to holding hands, hugging and gentle kissing. This affection, in turn, creates a strong intimacy. People, in general, have different sexual preferences. A healthy relationship does not mean that the couple makes love on a daily basis. It also does not exclude this as a possibility. What it does mean is that both partners enjoy this intimacy. This deep bond exists due to the friendship that is present. This friendship is like no other, and it is vital. A healthy relationship means that both partners enjoy each other's company. They have fun, they confide in each other, and they keep each other's secrets. It is, in fact, the connection that makes a healthy relationship possible.

Understanding and support.

Understand the needs of your partner. Your partner's needs are different from yours. Understand and appreciate these needs and do your best to satisfy the ones you can.

Self-love and self-respect.
Love yourself first. You need to love yourself first before loving your partner. It is okay to be selfish sometimes in a relationship. Find your happiness from within. The worst mistake you can make in a relationship is to rely on your partner to be happy in life. You will always find yourself unhappy, because he or she may not give you all the happiness you may need.

Positive and realistic attitude.
Take it easy. There is nothing that is so serious in this life. Also, do not expect too much from your partner.

For a relationship to exist, the couple must love each other. In some cases, unfortunately, people exist together but are not committed. It is this commitment that defines a relationship. All loving couples should strive to be as healthy and happy as possible. A healthy relationship is one which gets better in time, with growing respect, communication and the ability to listen, honesty, trust and friendship. All these things are possible to be achieved with time and they will create a beautiful history. A strong couple looks at this history with joy, not regret.

For any couple to be healthy, both partners need to work on this. This work, on its own, is the embodiment of a healthy relationship. This mutual wish to make each other better and be proud of each other is what helps couples to be happy. In summary, it is possible for people to stop their abusiveness, regain control and build a healthy and fulfilling relationship. However, this takes discipline, understanding and hard work.

WHEN YOU LEAVE A TOXIC PARTNER BEHIND: MOVING FORWARD AND A PATH TO RECOVERY

As discussed in previous chapters, if you are in a relationship that's negatively impacting your mental, physical or emotional health, or compromising your inner values, hurting others you love, you're likely in a toxic relationship – and the addictive neural patterns are in control.

By their nature, toxic relationships are filled with emotional drama that is designed to manipulate a certain result by the people creating it. Because the emotional drama is so severe, it undermines rational behavior and also inflicts intense emotional stress, which can have lasting traumatic effect - hence, the word "toxic." If you haven't already, take time to reflect on the dynamics of your toxic relationship, and to consider what you can and cannot do – this will enable you to break free of your partner's control, and to also take charge of your emotional response, so that your body and mind might restore balance and begin the healing process.

A toxic relationship can be one of the most emotionally taxing things that we can experience. They leave us feeling angry, worrisome, drained and stressed. If you do find yourself involved with a psychopath or someone who doesn't want to change or abuses you sexually or physically, it's best to leave such a partner as soon as possible. No love is worth risking your own health, well-being or even life. Because a toxic relationship can be so overwhelming and feel so incredibly confusing emotionally, you might feel like there's no way that you can ever be able to truly heal.

Here are the necessary steps to heal and recover after ending your toxic relationship.

1. Be completely honest with yourself.
Allow yourself to be disgusted with the individual for how they treated you. Cry - you'll cry a lot. Do not blame yourself. You have been through enough emotional pain and you are most likely feeling quite exhausted. You should encourage yourself and be confident in the fact that you're leaving your partner for your own well-being – so that you can truly be happy.

2. Prepare to go over all or some stages of grief.
You will not sleep, you will not eat, you may have to take time off work, so that you can deal with your emotions, you will most likely cry yourself to sleep for a while. There's nothing you can do about any of these, except keep going until it is over with.

3. Once the toxic relationship is over, stop all contact with former toxic partner.
Stop calling, texting and leave them alone; don't answer their calls or texts either. Cut them off completely. Don't enable them to try to contact you again. Completely block the toxic person out of your life. Do whatever you have to do. Sometimes, particularly when you are hurting, if you do it respectfully it can give you a sense of power. So, if you cannot be blunt to your partner about why you are leaving or

you are having trouble ending the relationship, then turn it around and push it until you've manipulated them into saying it. If they are toxic and intentionally trying to hurt you, it will not take long until they make a threat to end the relationship – and then go with it, stick with it and do not look back.

4. Don't worry about their feelings.

Toxic people do not have the same feelings as us! Well… they are capable to feel some emotions, however, as far as you are concerned from now on, they aren't. Think about how long they have disregarded your feelings. Why is this important? Because if you consider the toxic person's feelings, you will continue with your self-doubt and might go back. If you ever find yourself with some level of concern for somebody who's hurting you, stop and focus on the fact that you are important and deserve better than your present circumstances. Believe that this will lead you to a better reality – it might mean sitting with the emotional pain for some time, but in the end it will certainly be worth it. Anything is better than having to go back and suffer because of a toxic relationship again.

5. Do not try to replace the toxic person.

They say the fastest way to get over someone is to find someone new. This is not the case when you are trying to recover from a toxic relationship. When you are recovering from a relationship that's toxic, unfortunately, you are exceptionally vulnerable, more than if you are just recovering from a normal break up. There's a high chance that you'll entice another toxic individual into your life. Do not go with it. Take comfort in knowing that if the person has left you for somebody else, the chances that they are truly happy or will be happy in the long-term are quite slim. And you would certainly have left them anyway due to the fact that the relationship was toxic. If you were the one to leave, stick firm to your decision.

6. Accept that your time was wasted and the relationship was fake.

Realize that no matter what the person said or did, the relationship was not real. If it was real and you had recognized that it was toxic for you – well, there is no way any rational individual should be in such a relationship in the first place. So they can say whatever they like, but the whole relationship was fake. Do not give the toxic person the satisfaction of thinking the relationship would be real, if you had known the real circumstances. Deep down they know that the relationship was fake as well, otherwise they would certainly have come clean about any deception at the beginning.

7. Detox yourself as much as possible.

Be strong! Remove anything that might remind you of the toxic relationship from your life. Get rid of any letters, photos, gifts and anything that might remind you of that person. Delete their e-mails. Delete their telephone number. Lose their address and bag up everything that you want to return to them and be done with it. You should go on extensive, destructive, deleting mission. By the end of it you'll feel as though the toxic relationship is just …. deleted! Don't get me wrong: you will not feel good, you will not feel satisfied, you will definitely not get your smile back for some time, but it's less painful than having to look back and remember.

8. Commit to focusing on taking care of you.

Make your own self-care a daily commitment. Begin every day with a prayer or meditation. Do yoga. Go for a daily walk or run out in nature. Pay attention to your diet, eat more veggies and fruits and less processed foods. It's also important that you start a practice of checking in with your body regularly. Before you sit down to eat a meal or when you notice that you are stressed, you should stop and focus on your body and then ask yourself "How does my body feel?" Because of our body's natural fight or flight response, it naturally reacts when we experience worry, anger, and general stress. The more we take the time to stop and tune in and ask ourselves how our body feels, the easier it is to calm down and find peace.

9. Seek out support.

Unfortunately, there's no way to fast track your way through dealing with the pain. This is due to the fact that toxic relationships are emotionally draining. Many abuse survivors suffer from post-traumatic stress (though not all post-traumatic stress rises to the level of being diagnosed as a "disorder"). After being in a toxic relationship, it is natural to have your sense of trust and safety shaken. You may also feel confused and "feel like" you have become paranoid. This is one of the common features of post-traumatic stress. Nature has us wired in such a way that whenever we experience traumatic events, we become hyper vigilant and hypersensitive with regard to things that are closely associated with the trauma. Hence it takes a lot of counter-conditioning to weaken the painful bonds that developed between the traumatic events we experienced in the toxic relationship and our emotional responses to them. This is a natural protection mechanism. Only when we have sorted out all the reasons for the trauma and fairly and adequately assessed our ability to cope, can we be able to care for ourselves and love again.

It is very important that you find some support system when you are trying to learn how to cope. See a good life coach, psychologist or psychotherapist (preferably who specializes in domestic violence and relationships). You should also make a pact with somebody you really trust and love, that you'll not be in touch with the toxic person ever again. This means, although you are vulnerable, you will be able to depend on the strength of other people. The most healthy, positive people are usually those who have experienced the most painful moments in life themselves. They have lost and grieved, and they know what it is like to be hurt by somebody that is close to you. Connect to positive people, learn from their experience and advice and believe that one day you will be the most healthy, positive person you can be.

10. Stay hopeful for the future.

The breakup happened for a good reason and you are not meant to be with that person. Although you might be hurting now, your pain will eventually go away and you will be healthy, happy, and whole again. Do not lose hope for your future health, happiness, love and relationships! Know that your ex taught you valuable life lessons you needed to learn, but now it is time to move on in peace, confidence and hope.

FREQUENTLY ASKED QUESTIONS

1. **I am in a relationship with a toxic partner. Should I stay and try to improve it or should I leave?**

There's no firm rule to follow, but these are the general recommendations to keep in mind: analyse your relationship and have a heart-to-heart discussion with your partner about their willingness to work on themselves and change their behavioural patterns. Needless to say, if you are a victim of domestic abuse, contact authorities, seek professional help and end the relationship.

2. **I have been a victim of physical domestic abuse but I'm scared to go the police or even let anyone know. I feel like I provoked my partner myself.**

First of all, you should never be physically assaulted by your partner, no matter what you do or say. If that happens and your partner shows little to no remorse, seek help immediately. You might be risking your health or even life! If you still don't want police to get involved, go to your family, friends or relatives. Get out of the house and take care of your safety as soon as possible.

3. I can't afford professional help and my family/friends are not there for me.

If you are a victim of sexual or physical domestic abuse, use the resources of the Commission on Domestic and Sexual Violence (The National Domestic Violence Pro Bono Directory). Here you can find free legal representation. (web-site below in the Resources section).

Also, you can contact The National Domestic Violence Hotline, 1-800-799-SAFE (7233) or 1-800-787-3224 (TTY). Their highly trained advocates are available 24/7 to talk confidentially with anyone experiencing domestic violence, seeking resources or information, or questioning unhealthy aspects of their relationship.

HelpGuide.org – is a non-profit guide to mental health and well-being has a lot of resources and information on how to get out of an abusive relationship, how to protect your privacy, where to turn for help, find shelters, etc.

Please also take a look at some national organizations listed in the Resources section.

4. My partner has agreed to work on his/her behavioral issues and abusive patterns but I don't see any real changes. How can I know if he/she is really trying to change or just lying to keep me longer in this relationship?

Look out for the following signs that your partner is not changing:

- Continues to blame others for their behaviour.
- Makes additional demands in exchange for getting help.
- Insists that you are the one who needs counselling or you are the one who's provoking his/hers abusive attitude.
- Is willing to start/continue treatment only if you stay in the relationship.
- Tries to get sympathy from your family, friends, loved ones, and even you.

5. I'm afraid I'm being tracked. How can I protect my privacy?

There are a few important suggestions to keep in mid. Try to use landline as opposed to a cell phone – it's more difficult to tap and track. Use a pre-paid card whenever possible. Make sure to put a pass lock on your cell phone and keep it with you at all times. Check your cell phone settings to make sure you don't have tracking applications installed and also disable "GPS" when not in use. Some domestic violence shelters even offer free cell phones to women. When you go online to seek help, use a computer outside your home when possible. Apple store has laptops you can use if needed. Go to your friends or family members. Also change all your usernames and passwords to make sure your partner can't log in under your name. It goes without saying that you should avoid using birthdays, nicknames, etc. as your log in credentials.

Consider also the fact that you might be spied on. Your partner doesn't need fancy surveillance cameras as the "nanny cam" or baby monitor will work just fine. GPS devices are also easy to use nowadays and can be hidden anywhere, including your car. If you spot the device, do not move or disable it under any circumstances until you're ready to leave your abuser. Otherwise, this will alert them that you are aware of being spied on and might put you in danger.

6. I left my partner but I still don't feel safe and fear that he/she might find me to get revenge for leaving.

This is a very natural and understandable reaction. Listen to your gut, however, don't become overly paranoid. To make sure your abuser doesn't find you after you leave, change your phone number, consider using a P.O. Box rather than home address for your mail for the time being, research and apply to your state's address confidentiality program – a service that confidentially forwards your mail to your home; cancel your credit cards and close your bank accounts; open new ones with a new bank.

If you suspect that your former partner may be stocking you, consider getting a restraining order. In any case, always keep your cell phone with you to be ready to call the police if needed. But remember, a restraining order doesn't guarantee your full safety and protection. It can only be enforced if it's violated. To learn more about how they work, call The National Domestic Violence Hotline, 1-800-799-SAFE (7233).

Thank you for reading!

Please do me a favor: share your thoughts if you enjoyed this book!

REFERENCES

1. American Psychiatric Association. Diagnostic and Statistical Manual of Mental Disorders, Fourth Edition, Revised.

2. Do Personality Testing http://dopersonalitytest.com

3. M. Stout, Ph.D. "The Sociopath Next Door: The Ruthless Versus The Rest Of Us"

4. http://www.columbia.edu/~da358/npi16/npi16_jrp.pdf

5. http://www.thehotline.org/is-this-abuse/healthy-relationships/

6. http://girlshealth.gov/relationships/healthy/index.html

7. http://www.huffingtonpost.com/robert-weiss/how-much-sex-is-healthy_b_4214472.html

8. http://www.mayoclinic.org/diseases-conditions/narcissistic-personality-disorder/basics/complications/con-20025568

9. http://www.theneurotypical.com/posttraumatic_relationship_syndrome.html

RESOURCES

1. http://www.helpguide.org
2. http://www.thehotline.org
3. ACOG Violence Against Women Department
4. Asian Task Force Against Domestic Violence
5. Battered Women's Justice Project
6. Break the Cycle
7. Corporate Alliance to End Partner Violence
8. FaithTrust Institute
9. Futures Without Violence
10. HopeLine from Verizon Wireless
11. Institute for Law and Justice
12. Joyful Heart Foundation
13. Legal Momentum
14. Legal Resource Center on Violence Against Women
15. Legal Services Corporation
16. loveisrespect
17. National Center on Domestic and Sexual Violence
18. The National Coalition Against Domestic Violence
19. National Sexual Violence Resource Center
20. National Suicide Prevention Lifeline
21. NO MORE
22. Peace Over Violence
23. US Department of Justice: Office on Violence Against Women | Domestic Violence State Coalitions
24. VAWnet
25. WomensLaw
26. YWCA

NOTES

NOTES

Printed in Great Britain
by Amazon